S0-AWR-770

CARS OF CUBA

CARS OF CUBA

Essay by Cristina Garcia
Photographs by Joshua Greene
Created by DD Allen

Harry N. Abrams, Inc., Publishers

Frontispiece: '58 Studebaker Silver Hawk on the Malecón, Havana

Editor: Eric Himmel
Designer: Raymond P. Hooper

Library of Congress Cataloging-in-Publication Data

Garcia, Cristina, 1958–
Cars of Cuba / essay by Cristina Garcia ; photographs by Joshua
Greene ; created by DD Allen.
p.   cm.
ISBN 0–8109–2631–8 (paperback)
1. Automobiles—Cuba. 2. Cuba—Social life and customs.
I. Greene, Joshua. II. Allen, DD III. Title.
TL33.C83G37 1995

629.222'097291—dc20   95-5434

Text copyright © 1995 Cristina Garcia
Photographs copyright © 1995 DD Allen

Published in 1995 by Harry N. Abrams, Incorporated, New York
All rights reserved. No part of the contents of this book may be reproduced
without the written permission of the publisher

Printed and bound in Hong Kong

CONTENTS

'52 Chevrolet Styleline Deluxe with Powerglide transmission at the Hotel Nacional, Havana

CACHARROS

CRISTINA GARCIA

There is a name for the gorgeous old American cars that continue to hum, rattle, and roll through the Cuban landscape: *cacharros*. Normally the word means a broken down jalopy that requires its owner to push it up bumps in the road. But in the case of these Yankee beauties—the white '49 Plymouth convertible at Varadero Beach, the eggplant-colored '52 Chevy Styleline Deluxe before the Hotel Nacional, the sleek black '59 Fleetwood Cadillac with minor roles in major motion pictures—cacharro is whispered softly, tenderly, like the name of a lost first love.

When Fidel Castro marched into Havana on New Year's Day of 1959, nearly thirty-five years ago, he could not have imagined that his triumph would ultimately create the greatest living American car museum in the world, a hunk of Americana not even available in the United States. But the severance of relations between Cuba and the U.S. in 1961 virtually assured the preservation of these marvelous mechanical dinosaurs. Cut off from the supplies and automotive evolution of the mainland, the cars, like any transplanted and isolated species, were forced to adapt. Flash frozen and tinkered with to perfection by Cuban mechanics legendary for their ingenuity and expertise, these automobiles are heroic testaments to their era: a time when gas was cheap and plentiful, the Space Age was imminent, and the future—if you didn't look too far into the atomic horizon—was so bright, you had to wear (3D) shades. How else to explain those fabulous, faux-aerodynamic, wildly fun and flared-out fins?

In Cuba, these grande dame Packards, Oldsmobiles, Lincolns, Buicks, De Sotos, Dodges, Pontiacs, Hudsons, Studebakers, Cadillacs, Fords, and ever-present Chevys are pampered and fussed over like first grandchildren. Their owners are unabashedly passionate about them. They make declarations of *amor* one would expect more from lovesick adolescents than burly grease-creased mechanics. The cars are buffed and polished, patched up and troubleshot, intestinally reconstituted with parts from Russian jeeps, trucks, and motorcycles until the owners wake up one fine Saturday morning reveling in the sounds they love to hear: vrooom, purrr, roar, mmmmmmm. It's working! They save up for gas, wait endlessly in lines for a few liters at best, and then: *Silvia! Pepito! Manolo! María! Get dressed! We're going for a ride!*

Un paseito. A little ride. That is all most of these gas-guzzlers can go for these days. Even with more fuel-efficient carburetors torn from Volkswagens or Russian Ladas, even with the most brilliant mechanics on the face of this blue-green planet, they cannot self-manufacture gas. Until recently, Cubans were allowed only about forty liters (roughly ten gallons) a month, down from 300 liters a month in 1991. This does not get them far; maybe to the next province for the obligatory visit to the in-laws on Sundays. Maybe for one blow-out drive to Havana or Varadero Beach. Maybe only for the month's essential errands. They bargain, trade, save, cajole as much gas as they can on the black market (going price: ninety

José de la Paz's '49 De Soto, Pinar del Río

U.S. cents a liter, which comes to about $3.40/gallon), or from friends of friends, or contacts in the government, or the "industry"—and then they're off! Freedom, wind, the open road, at least for an hour.

Every Cuban, the saying goes, is a mechanic. One wonders if this trait is born of necessity or is somehow genetically coded, like a propensity for *cafecito* so sweet it makes your teeth ache. Everyone who owns a vintage American *cacharro* in Cuba seems to know how to fix it. These men (it is always men) gather in their neighborhoods after work, fixing and tinkering, swapping tips like kerchiefed housewives from another epoch. This is their social gathering, their kaffee klatsch without the kaffee, the one place they don't have to worry about meeting quotas, pleasing their boss, or being good Communists. This is not work but leisure of the purest kind, undiluted joy.

Very few of these *cacharros* are one hundred percent original. While the degree of originality is prized—*Mira, señora,* they crow, taking your elbow and leading you to the treasure . . . a smooth, dentless chassis, perfectly preserved upholstery, two-tone paint as bright as the spring day in 1957 when it was applied—the ingenuity in adapting replacement parts is what separates the men from the boys. Despite the many advances of women in Cuba, despite the Family Code of 1975, *machismo* still reigns under the palms. And there is nothing quite so macho as bringing to life one of these goddesses.

José de la Paz, a retired mechanic in Pinar del Río province, boasts that the engine in his cream and pink '49 De Soto is so perfect that it doesn't burn oil. Okay, maybe just the tiniest amount, barely enough to grease a skillet. But no way could you fry plantains. De la Paz, who bought the automobile brand new for 2,500 pesos from the Dodge agency in Havana, was recently offered 40,000 pesos for it. He indignantly refused. His De Soto hasn't needed a repair since 1984. What would he do with the money, anyway? In Cuba, for Cubans at least, there was, until recently, no place to spend the cash. Besides, he's nicely rigged up the radio to run from a battery in the trunk. And, oh yes, in case you haven't noticed, his house is painted the exact same colors as his car.

But don't think for a moment that these automobiles are treated like delicate hothouse orchids. Most are not hermetically sealed in temperature-controlled security garages the way they would be in the U.S. These cacharros, whenever humanly possible, are put to work. They are exotic cash cows, a source of foreign exchange. Good for tourists and tours, weddings and *quince* celebrations. No underemployment here. Go to any big resort hotel on the island and you'll see these beauties parked in the lots, one after another, shining like so many sun reflectors. Dare to walk by them. Something primal and indescribable will force your hand into your pocket. Twenty dollars buys gas enough for a decent spin. Seventy dollars gets you a day in a top-of-the-line Cadillac convertible with fins so big they block the rear view mirror. Forget about renting from Hertz or Avis ever again.

Filmmakers from around the world feature the *crème de la crème* of these automobiles in movies, television shows, and commercials. The owners get paid in hard currency, which is what everyone in Cuba is after. Dollars, francs, and deutsche marks are their ticket, if not to the good life, then to a better, more comfortably upholstered one. A few well-placed dollars go a long way on the island, secure little luxuries like toilet paper or seafood or hammers obtainable no other way. One woman, offered a bar of Ivory soap in exchange for a photograph of her '57 Ford, burst into tears of gratitude.

Lily Galainena, an enterprising *viejita* of seventy-plus years, drives foreign visitors on architectural tours of her beloved Havana in a '53 Chevrolet. Another gentleman, the owner of a spectacular white '55 Cadillac convertible, charges four hundred pesos for a wedding in his hometown of Cotorro, nine hundred for nuptials in the capital. Along the Malecón, that sweet curve of road where Havana meets the sea, the Rum Boys are cruising big time in a sleek '50 Chevy. Despite the fact that the car belongs to one of their mothers, they are genuine bad boys, the kind everyone else's mother warns you about. They're draped inside the cacharro with studied nonchalance, hustling up rides for a bottle of rum. If they manage to score, say from crazy Canadian tourists wanting a spin in their car, they disappear for days, too soused to drive.

Tito Lazaro Vilela also makes a good living from his '59 Mercury. He used to drive a truck before the gas ran out and his salary was cut to seventy-five pesos a month. Tito's extended family put their heads together and decided to trade their rundown

'55 Cadillac, Cotorro

Tito Lazaro Vilela's '59 Mercury Montclair at Marina Hemingway, Havana

'56 Chevrolet plus 36,000 scrounged-together pesos for the pristine Mercury. The investment has paid off. This one car, this Yankee anachronism, this flamboyant product of fat cat American corporatism, is keeping the Vilela tribe in Cuba happily fed and clothed three and a half decades after it bumped off the assembly line in Detroit. Talk about capitalist tools.

Tourists are not the only ones smitten by these dazzling behemoths, although in many ways the rising influx of tourists during the last decade has sparked a renewed appreciation of the American cacharros. For a while in the 1980s, the Cuban government attempted to cash in on the vintage cars in Europe, North America, and Japan by buying up as many of the local cacharros as possible. In exchange, they promised owners a brand new (and widely scorned) Russian Lada. The dearth of parts and gas forced many a heartbreaking decision. After all, to many families, their cacharros were family. How could they turn in their automotive *abuelitas* for mere transportation? Cuban officials collected the cars on huge lots, enticing foreigners starved for a little felicitous form in a world gone to hell with function. Many of the island's best automobiles left the tropics in this desperate bid for foreign exchange. The exodus came to an abrupt halt in 1989 when the government discovered its apparatchiks diverting profits into their own pockets.

❋

What is it about these cars that makes the hearts of even confirmed subway riders do a little cha-cha-chá in the chest? Is it that irresistible stretch of grinning grillwork? Those low-slung trunks you want to throw luggage into? Those acres of chrome, hoarding a hog's share of sunlight? In the early 1950s, car stylists actually measured chrome by the square inch, making sure they had enough. Longer, lower, wider. That was the ethos of the day. Gadgets like flip-up gas fillers, push-button gear selectors, and swivel seats became de rigueur. Automobiles, more than ever, became blatant extensions of the personality. Sex was linked to horsepower. The boxy models of the thirties and forties gave way to a potent new curvaceousness. Dr. Jean Rosenbaum, a well-known psychiatrist of the time, pronounced that for men: "See what a big car I have," could be translated as "See what a big penis I have (or wish I had)."

So *that's* what this is all about? In a world where sex can be scary and four-cylinder cars rumble out of international factories with a ho-

'55 Ford and two '55 Thunderbirds at the Cubalse lot, Cubanacán, Havana

hum gumdrop likeness, these old cacharros positively explode with a riotous sensuality. Get within ten yards of one and it is impossible, literally impossible, to keep your hands to yourself. You close your eyes and take in the catch and growl of the motor. You open them and follow those sinuous lines like silver trajectories to your past and future. You yearn for a letter sweater and a chocolate malt to share with your sweetheart. (So what if she just deserted you and you never played sports? So what if you grew up in Manhattan and failed your driving test nine times?) You slip in behind the steering wheel. Suddenly you understand why you were born. Stop everything. Find some gas. Let's drive this baby to Santiago!

In Cuba, it's that way for everyone: a cacharro with a working battery and a full tank of gas is a holiday in itself. Forget Christmas. Forget Carnival. Forget the Forty-First Anniversary of Fidel's Attack on the Moncada Barracks. It's party time! Somehow, through a dizzying chain of bartering, string pulling, and back slapping, the fixings for a cook-out materialize. Twelve people of assorted length and girth climb into a just-resuscitated '49 Plymouth convertible and head straight for the beach. The water is bath warm, the wind stirs just enough to keep the mosquitoes disoriented, and the radio blasts a salsa so hot it nearly overcooks the pork. *Sí, hombre, así vivímos.*

Public transportation, a necessary evil, just doesn't cut it. Neither do the tin cans-on-wheels from the ex-Soviet bloc. Emilio Fernández understands this. He owns three cacharros himself—a Dodge, a Ford, and a Chevy, all from the forties and fifties—but only one working battery. A Mother Teresa among mechanics, Emilio lends this single battery to fellow cacharro owners stranded with dead batteries. One neighbor needs it to go visit his mother for her birthday (heaven help him if he doesn't show up). Another wants to take his family on a long-delayed trip to another province. Emilio always obliges. His is the pure spirit of the Revolution.

To repair a cacharro in Cuba you need:
A) imagination
B) connections, and
C) mucho chutzpah.

You can't just walk into an automotive store or drive up to a reputable garage and request a new muffler or a brake job. If you are sufficiently unenlightened to actually take your car to a state-run repair shop, you might as well bid farewell to the decent parts you do have. Theft is a big problem both inside and outside the official garages. Cars are stripped for parts or stolen for illegal resale. Consequently, many of the finest cacharros are kept under tarpaulins, a sure sign that there is something underneath worth stealing. Some car owners have gone so far as to inscribe their initials on the windshields in a vague attempt at security. It doesn't stop the crooks.

The black market for spare parts, especially old American spare parts, is enormous and highly lucrative. The market's machinations are a mystery to all but the initiated. Yet the persistent (and Cubans are nothing if not persistent) can always find a way to tap into the network. One man, the owner of a white Studebaker, complained that some *desgraciado* had stolen the tail lights right off his car. His annoyance was tempered somewhat by the fact that he'd heard there was a source in Viñales, 130 miles west of Havana, who might be able to supply him with another set, possibly original. That is how he would spend his Sunday.

When a repair problem goes beyond the talents of a particular car owner and his little neighborhood group, the names of brilliant mechanics around the country are reverentially whispered. There are usually a couple of these men in every province, übermechanics in a land of technical aces. Men whose thick, blackened hands should be enshrined along with other totems of the Revolution. Men whose miracles of mechanical verve and inventiveness render fellow craftsmen weak with admiration. Outside their country, they might be hopelessly lost in a world of all-electronic ignitions, air bags, anti-lock brakes, and automatic cruise control. But in Cuba, their services are absolutely required. These mechanics usually work out of their homes, on the sly, charging exorbitant fees for exorbitant solutions. No one begrudges them a centavo.

Others get around car trouble by machining their own parts. Antonio Aguilera of Santiago de Cuba converted his garage into a sideline business producing parts for American automobiles. It is as much a labor of love as profit since he, too, is the owner of a beautiful cacharro—a '56 Hudson Hornet Hollywood, green and white with yellow trim, so perfect it could suck nectar from wildflowers. A familiar scene: Aguilera is reviving a dead cacharro for an increasingly restless group of young men. They mill about, drinking beer, looking over Aguilera's shoulder. It's getting later and later and there's a party somewhere. The prettiest girls will already

be taken. Suddenly, the engine springs to life. Cheers break out all around. Before they can hail Aguilera a genius, they're halfway down the road.

The scarcity of original parts has forged thousands of exotic mechanical marriages. Russian Gaz jeeps are particularly sought after for parts since their engines were copied from an American engine and adapt very nicely to many cacharros of the fifties. The Lada's carburetor, while no gem by any stretch of the imagination, is frequently grafted inside vintage American cars to improve mileage in gas-lean times. Organ donations from Volkswagens and other vehicles also come to the rescue of the cacharros. Rigoberto Ramírez Pérez of Havana cannibalized an entire Ford Falcon to resurrect a blue '36 Chevy. He and others on the island do what they can with the limited resources at hand. Who says the spirit of sacrifice is dead in revolutionary Cuba?

One hears of beer cans doubling as pistons (although no one ever admits to actually having seen this with his own two eyes). "Bolts" made of baling wire apparently are not uncommon. Cuban exiles in Miami sneer that it is the paper clips they left behind years ago that keep the body and soul of these cars intact. Mechanics in Cuba repeat the same joke with a certain amount of pride. One thing is certain: long before the Cold War thawed, cubanos were employing their own practical form of mechanical détente.

Paint is nearly as hard to get as spare parts. One year, pink may be all that's available—not a decorous pastel pink but a Tropicana showgirl neon pink—and suddenly, it seems, every car

Opposite: Pedro Pérez Vega's '57 Ford Custom 300, Carretera Viñales

in the capital is in flamingo drag. Some cars have had so many paint jobs that a minor amount of sanding and scraping yield peeling frescoes of confetti colors.

Cubans also love to gussy up their cacharros with a myriad of knick-knacks and decorations that would horrify purist vintage car owners anywhere else. In Cuba, historic preservation is a luxury few can afford. Sleek hood ornaments (streamlined birds in takeoff positions are particular favorites) are traded and mounted and extolled. Painted flames arch back from front wheels. Flashy metallic stars, made by local artisans, are frequently bolted to the sides of the automobiles. Blue glass side windows turn backseats into soothing sanctuaries. Mercedes-Benz emblems ironically adorn the dashboards of many garden-variety Chevrolets. And stickers of all sorts enliven even the most beat-up cacharros with a little humor: T-U-R-B-O-C-H-A-R-G-E they scream across the windshield. Yeah, right.

It is a shock to learn how many cacharros are still in the hands of their original owners, or have been passed down from one generation to the next like cherished family heirlooms. Pedro Pérez Vega, of Pinar del Río province, bought his blue and white '57 Ford brand new. In all these years he's put only 140,000 miles on it. He stores it under a thatched roof carport and swears it's never given him more than a half-day of trouble. Manuel Mario Aguilera also bought his '50 Oldsmobile direct from an American dealer. He estimates its mileage at 400,000 miles. Reading odometers is not a precise business in Cuba. ¿Quién, carajo, se recuerda? Does it really matter how many times the thing's gone around? The car is running, isn't it? Rolando Urquiola, a Havana mechanic, inherited his immaculate '51 Chevy from his father, also a mechan-

ic. He claims it is the best-maintained car on the island. It is impossible to doubt him.

Cacharros are the quintessential ice breakers in contemporary Cuba. People who might otherwise be too shy or frightened to speak with foreigners turn positively garrulous when it comes to their beloved antediluvians. There is none of the usual looking over the shoulder to see who might be watching or listening to their conversation. They give their names freely and do not fear repercussions. When they praise their cacharros, owners lose track of time, superlatives, anecdotes. They engage in fleecy reminiscences. Boasting is part of the good-natured fun of it all.

When the maitre d' at the Hotel Nacional, once the swankiest hotel in Havana, bought his Chevrolet Deluxe Power Glide in 1952, he claims it was one of three cars in Cuba that had air conditioning. He had the world by the tail in those days, driving around with his windows rolled all the way up. He never had any trouble giving a good-looking woman a ride. Forty-two years later, the air conditioning still works perfectly. And women still point at him, impressed.

Cubans love having their cars photographed. One owner of a black '38 Buick became so excited at the prospect of having his fifty-five-year-old baby immortalized in this book that he worked two days straight getting it running again. Even his wife got all dressed up for the big event. Others proudly recount their cars' milestones like parents of precocious children. The owner of a navy-and-white '59 Dodge Coronet gleefully relates how his automobile has already "killed" two Russian Ladas. It is clear he expects the death toll to climb.

Car homicides aside, there is virtually no overt politicization of

'38 Buick with original engine, original upholstery, and Lada speedometer, Iglesia de San Francisco de Paola, Havana

these vehicles. Although many of the vintage car owners are certainly intrigued by America, their interest, more often than not, happens to coincide with a love for the cars, but it is not necessarily connected to it. Yet there is something of a residual emotional link to the United States, especially among the older generation of cacharro owners. Is it possible, after all, to be in love with such an unmistakable icon of America without feeling the slightest stir for its popular culture?

Hector Fernández and his family live in a graceful old mansion in the Miramar section of Havana. Fernández, an avid disciple of General Motors, keeps his three vintage cars, a '50 Chevy, a '55 Olds, and a '56 Dodge, in impeccable condition by the courtyard fountain. He bought the cars in happier times. These days, his family is ostracized for having applied for a visa to leave the country for Panama. His son-in-law, Rodolfo, a lunatic Yankees fan and former world-class marathoner, has been demoted to teaching running to elementary school children. Rodolfo's son, Steve (he insists on being called Steve, not Estéban), is mad for Jack Nicholson. The family has erected a shrine to the actor—an autographed glossy obtained through an American friend is the centerpiece—in a corner of the living room, right over the ancient television set. It is one of their most prized possessions.

The Cuban government seems oblivious to the irony and symbolism of having all these American fossils revving up their motors under its nose. In fact, several of the more famous American cacharros are displayed in a museum dedicated to automobiles that have played a prominent role in the Revolution, like the car that Raúl Castro, Fidel's brother, drove during the attack on the Moncada barracks in 1953. Or the Maximum Leader's mother's Ford. Although the car's contribution is not specified, one is tempted to speculate how Cuba's history might have changed if Alina Ruz had driven, say, a Peugeot. Another vintage car, a '56 Buick Special, stands as a monument to all the heroic *compañeros* of Santiago who died fighting for the Revolution. People actually make pilgrimages to these cars, bearing wreaths and roses. There is no tongue-in-cheek involved.

Pilgrimages of another sort occur among the cacharro owners themselves. Many make a hobby or holiday out of visiting the finest vintage American automobiles on the island. Invariably, those with great cars know or have heard, at least, of everyone else with a great car. They've seen each other driving around town, worked together on movies or televisions shows, thumbed the pictures taken by fellow enthusiasts on cross-country trips.

In fact, something of a cacharro hierarchy has developed in this socialist land. In the absence of Jaguars, BMWs, and Lexuses, the old fifties order still dominates. The owners of good Cadillacs are the elite, the automotive royalty. A '59 Eldorado Biarritz convertible—with fins that could slice the island in two—is as desirable a camp classic in Cuba as it is in the United States. (Perhaps it is no coincidence, then, that the Revolution was ushered in at the height of this stylistic excess. Subsequent years saw the fins devolve into smaller and smaller appendages—mere scales, really—before disappearing altogether. A more sobering age was dawn-

Opposite: The Rum Boys' '50 Chevrolet Styleline on the Malecón, Havana

ing on both sides of the Straits of Florida.)

General Motors cars are prized next after Cadillacs. Ask any cacharro owner in Cuba who made the best American cars before 1960 and the response, invariably, is GM. Now they may have an oddball or sentimental favorite, like the '53 Studebaker Starlight Coupe, one of the most sensational-looking cars ever built. But this has nothing to do with engineering. Studebakers are referred to locally as Studedesgracias, which translates roughly as: "Sure they look nice, but forget about going anywhere."

In Cuba there are about ten General Motors cars for every three Chryslers and two Fords. Chevrolets are far and away the most popular, probably because they were the most affordable automobiles of their time exported to Cuba. Currently, there are 5,413 registered Chevys on the island, most of them '51 to '57 models. One wonders if other American accoutrements of the time also abound in long-forgotten drawers—saddle shoes and poodle skirts, Brylcreem and Elvis Presley's Sun recordings. Or was it all mambo mambo mambo fever?

Today, while Americans are squeezing themselves into stingy econo-boxes, Cubans, who have far less in material goods and certainly much less fuel, continue struggling to preserve these grandiose, octane-gobbling boats. Only in Cuba is the flagrance and pleasure of the American automobile phenomenon thoroughly savored—a direct expression of individuality in a sea of government conformity. The cars themselves have gone native in Cuba, thoroughly tropical, a little soft in the head from the heat. They're like a bunch of deliriously happy Michigan retirees in paradise, complete with daiquiris and tiny paper umbrellas. They have the best care in the world (Hell, with Cuban mechanics they'll live forever!), move around quite a bit for their age, and take in the sun with other old fogeys. What more could they possibly want?

Indisputably, the Cubans, over the years, have made these cars—these ultimate Yankee artifacts—their own. It's not just the multi-colored flags waving from the antennas, invoking the protection of Changó or Obatalá or another one of their favorite *santería* gods, or the little leather armrests that prevent blisters from too-hot chrome, but the Cubans' total reclamation of these automobiles. Sure, it's wonderful if the original tuck and roll is in good condition, but if not, old clothes or burlap sacking will do just fine—for now. What, there's no gas for the guzzler? Bueno, let's go around to that young gas station attendant's house and see if he can't sell us just the tiniest bit to get us going (many station attendants do a brisk black market business siphoning off a liter of gas here and there).

The truth of the matter is, that despite the restrictions and privations of their society, despite a future that promises only uniform goods and a constant shortage of them, despite highways overrun with those downright dowdy Ladas, there is still plenty of energy to worship these old cacharros. Perhaps it is only fitting that their owners hold the keys to these perfect American symbols of nostalgia and hope. Now if they could only get their hands on those few drops of gas . . .

—*Los Angeles, 1995*

Opposite: Rolando Urquiola's '52 Chevrolet Styleline, Havana Vieja

CARS OF CUBA

Juan Francisco Sita's '58 Ford Fairlane at the Parque Central, Havana Vieja

'56 Chevrolet One-Fifty at El Floridita, Havana Vieja

'48 Buick Roadmaster, Centro Havana

'53 Pontiac Chieftain, Viñales

Alberto Pérez's '53 Chrysler New Yorker, Vedado, Havana

'53 Buick Super, Vedado, Havana

'53 Chevrolet Bel Air at Miguelito's house, Viñales

'57 Dodge Coronet, Havana

'58 Plymouth Savoy, outside Havana

'53 Chevrolet Two-Ten Sport Coupe, outside Havana

Hector Fernández's '56 Dodge Coronet, Miramar, Havana

Hector Fernández's '57 Oldsmobile Golden Rocket Eighty-Eight, Miramar, Havana

'54 Cadillac Fleetwood, Vedado, Havana

'57 Ford Custom, Avenida del Puerto, Havana Vieja

'53 Chevrolet Bel Air, Vedado, Havana

Juan Carlos Martínez's '53 Chevy Two-Ten on the Malecón, Havana

'46 Chevrolet with '47 grille, Matanzas

Manuel Aguilera's '50 Oldsmobile Eighty-Eight (original color) on the Malecón, Havana

'55 Buick Roadmaster, outside Havana

Juan Carlo Gómez's '56 Chevrolet One-Fifty on the Malecón, Havana

Rafael's '59 Cadillac Fleetwood at the Cementerio de Colón, Vedado, Havana

'57 Cadillac Fleetwood at the Habana Riviera

Mario Vaque Borbolla's '47 Cadillac Fleetwood, Miramar, Havana

'56 Pontiac Star Chief, Vedado, Havana

'59 Dodge Coronet at the residence of the British Embassador, Vedado, Havana

'53 Ford Customline in Santa Fe after a storm

Antonio Aguilera's '56 Hudson Hornet Hollywood, Santiago de Cuba

'36 Chevrolet Standard Town Sedan, Plaza Vieja, Havana

Twelve people in a '58 Edsel, Jaimanitas, Havana

'54 Buick Skylark, Santiago de Cuba

'38 Packard being restored, Santiago de Cuba

'47 Buick, outside Havana

'56 Buick Special, outside Havana

'57 Rambler, Playa, Havana

'49 Chevrolet Styleline, Vedado, Havana

'50 Chevrolet Fleetline, Prehistoric Valley, Baconao Park

'48 Dodge, outside Varadero

'59 Dodge, outside Cárdenas

'49 Chevrolet Styleline, Viñales

'50 Ford Deluxe, outside Varadero

'55 Mercury Monterey, Plaza Vieja, Havana

'53 Chevrolet Two-Ten, outside Matanzas

'46 Ford Deluxe, Santiago de Cuba